THE *NEW KIDS'* QUESTION & ANSWER BOOK

© copyright 1993 Greey de Pencier Books
Books from OWL are published by Greey de Pencier Books, 56 The Esplanade, Suite 302, Toronto, Ontario M5E 1A7.

*OWL and the Owl colophon are trademarks of the Young Naturalist Foundation.
Greey de Pencier is a licensed user of trademarks of the Young Naturalist Foundation.

Published simultaneously in the United States by Firefly Books (U.S.) Inc.
P. O. Box 1338, Ellicott Station, Buffalo, NY 14205.

This book was published with the generous support of the Canada Council and the Ontario Arts Council.

Canadian Cataloguing in Publication Data
Main entry under title:

The New kids' question and answer book

Includes index.
ISBN 1-895688-05-1 (pbk.) - ISBN 1-895688-09-4 (bound)

1. Natural history - Miscellanea - Juvenile literature.
2. Science - Miscellanea - Juvenile literature.
I. Farris, Katherine.

QH48.N48 1993   j508   C93-093260-9

Art Director: Julia Naimska
Cover Photography: Dick Haneda

Special thanks to Debora Pearson, editor of OWL Magazine, Deena Waisberg, OWL's managing editor and
Tim Davin, OWL's art director, as well as to those contributing writers who worked with them in answering the questions:
Sheila Fairley, Katherine Farris, Linda Granfield, Susan Hughes, Jay Ingram, Elin Kelsey, Paula Kent Kuchmey, Bob Loeffelbein,
Elizabeth MacLeod, Cynthia Pratt Nicolson, Deena Waisberg, Lauren Wolk.

CONSULTANTS

Jeanne Byrne
Safe Energy Communication Council

Dick Cannings
Vertebrate Museum, Department of Zoology,
University of British Columbia

Dr. Kathy Coates
Department of Invertebrate Zoology,
Royal Ontario Museum

Jim Dick
Department of Ornithology,
Royal Ontario Museum

Terry Dickinson
Astronomy Consultant

Dr. Andrew Gordon
Department of Environmental Biology,
University of Guelph

Erling Holm
Department of Ichthyology and Herpetology,
Royal Ontario Museum

Dr. Sudhakar Joshi
Department of Physics, York University

Elin Kelsey
Vancouver Public Aquarium

Dr. Peter Kevan
Department of Environmental Biology,
University of Guelph

Colin Laird
Rocky Mountain Institute

Ross MacCulloch
Department of Ichthyology and Herpetology,
Royal Ontario Museum

Dr. Hooley McLaughlin
Ontario Science Centre

Dale Morris
Department of Entomology,
Royal Ontario Museum

Dr. Martin Moskovits
Department of Chemistry,
University of Toronto

Doug Reichle
California Energy Commission

Mary Ann Robinson
University of Guelph Greenhouse

George Simons
California Energy Commission

Thomas Spring
TLD Computers, Systems Consultant

Dr. Gerald Straley
U.B.C. Botanical Garden

David Tarrant
U.B.C. Botanical Garden

Patrick Tevlin
Ontario Science Centre

Dr. Wayne Weber
Wildlife Specialist, Crop Protection,
B.C. Ministry of Agriculture and Fisheries

Dr. Fred Wicks
Department of Minerology,
Royal Ontario Museum

Dr. Rick Winterbottom
Department of Ichthyology and Herpetology,
Royal Ontario Museum

Susan Woodward
Department of Mammology,
Royal Ontario Museum

PHOTOGRAPHY AND ILLUSTRATION CREDITS:

pp. 4 Gérard Lacz/NHPA; 5 (left) L. West/Nat'l Audubon Soc. Coll., P.R.; 5 Pat Stephens; 6 Nicholas Leibrecht; 6-7 Victor Gad; 7 D.S. Henderson/The Image Bank; 8-9 Julian Mulock; 10 (top) Tracy Walker; 10 Dan Hobbs; 11 Dan Hobbs; 12 (top) Jennifer Herbert; 12 Pat Cupples; 13 Dan Hobbs; 14 Tina Holdcroft; 15 Barbara Spurll; 17 Ray Boudreau; 18 Dan Hobbs; 19 (top) Michael McKinnell; 19 Canine Vision Canada; 20 David Scharf/Peter Arnold, Inc.; 21 (top) Tina Holdcroft; 21 Jock McRae; 22-23 Tim Young; 24-25 Pat Morrow/First Light; 25 Dan Hobbs; 26 (top) Kevin Ghiglione; 26 Sam Zarember/The Image Bank; 27 Thach Búi; 28-29 Donna Gordon; 30-31 Luiz Claudio Marigo/Peter Arnold, Inc.; 32 Pollution Probe; 33 Dan Hobbs; 34 Donna Gordon/"Energy Matters" booklet from the Ontario Ministry of Energy; 35 Scott Gwilliams/"Energy Matters" booklet from the Ontario Ministry of Energy; 36-37 G.I. Bernard/NHPA; 37 Marcos Sorensen; 38 © Danielle Jones; 38-39 Ray Boudreau; 39 Ray Boudreau; 40 Frank Viva; 41 Gary Clement; 42 L.West/ Nat'l Audubon Soc. Coll., P.R; 43 (top) John Cooke/ Oxford Scientific Films; 43 Pat Stephens; 44 Dan Hobbs; 45 Tim Gray/Wildlands League; 46 James L. Castner; 47 Julian Mulock; 48-49 Vesna Krstanovich; 50 Olena Kassian; 51 The Orangutan Foundation International; 52 (top) Kathy Boake/courtesy of Gifford Boake; 52 Dan Hobbs; 53 Ray Boudreau; 54 Frans Lanting/Minden; 55 Pat Stephens; 56-57 Tina Holdcroft; 58-59 Jock McRae; 60 Kevin Ghiglione; 61 Kennon Cooke/Valan Photos; 62-63 Jet Propulsion Laboratory/California Institute of Technology, National Aeronautics and Space Administration.

Printed in Hong Kong A B C D E F G

THE NEW KIDS' QUESTION & ANSWER BOOK

Questions Kids Ask About Nature, Science and the Environment

From the Editors of OWL Magazine

Compiled and Edited by Katherine Farris

Greey de Pencier Books

How do animals carry their babies?

◆

These babies don't need a ticket to travel first-class. Why? They rely on the Parent Express!

The Old Fold Hold

When a mother tiger needs to move quickly, she gently grabs her baby by the loose folds of skin on its neck. When she does this, her cub instinctively stops moving, probably to avoid being hurt. Why do tigers move their young? Usually to avoid being bothered or to avoid predators. But sometimes a mother must move her cub away from its father—male tigers have been known to eat their own young if they feel their territory is being threatened. A mother tiger isn't the only cat to carry her babies this way. Other wildcats also grab their young by the scruff of the neck. And if you think the tiger's way of carrying her babies is very familiar, take a look at a mother domestic cat. She'll do the same thing with her kittens . . . and it doesn't hurt a bit!

Was That a Burp or a Baby?

It takes a strong stomach to raise a family when you're a female gastric-brooding frog. This Australian amphibian swallows up to 20 fertilized eggs and leaves them in her stomach to develop. When they've grown into froglets, she vomits them up. Keeping them in her stomach means she can carry them with her easily wherever she goes, but there is one catch—as long as her babies are on the inside, the mother frog can't eat anything. There's sad news about this frog, though. None have been seen since the early 1980s. Scientists are worried that the frogs may have become extinct, although nobody is sure why.

The Portable Nest

Some birds spend a lot of time around the nest after their eggs have hatched. But not the grebe. As soon as its eggs have hatched, the grebe family heads for the water. Once there, both parents become floating nests, carrying the chicks on their backs. Riding up top protects the babies from water predators, like snapping turtles. And it's a great place to stay warm and dry.

Talk about Crowded!

This wolf spider might look fierce to you, but she is a very good mother to her 200 babies. She wraps her eggs in a protective cocoon and carries it around on her back. Then, once the young hatch, they spend another three weeks riding up top— stacked three layers deep!

How much does Earth weigh?

The answer to this question depends on what you mean by "weight." Often when people talk about weight, they mean the amount of matter in an object, or its mass. In the case of Earth, its mass is an unbelievable 6,000 million million million tonnes (tons). But when scientists talk about weight, they mean the force with which Earth's gravity pulls an object towards Earth. So really, Earth's weight can't be calculated because Earth itself causes gravity. You could say that Earth weighs nothing!

What is acid rain?

Acid rain is made when chemical gases—such as sulfur dioxide and nitrogen dioxide—from smoke stacks, metal smelters, power stations and car exhaust pipes are released into the sky. Carried by the winds, the gases mix with water in the air and are changed by sunlight into sulfuric or nitric acid. These acids then fall to the ground as acid rain or snow.

Acids can be weak or strong, but they all are able to eat away at things. The acids in acid rain are strong enough to gradually dissolve rocks, eat away buildings and bridges made of marble or limestone, burn the leaves of plants and trees, and dissolve the minerals in soil.

How acid is acid rain?

To find out how much acid there is in acid rain or snow, scientists use a pH scale, which measures acidity from 0 to 14. Anything below 7 is acidic. Rain is normally slightly acidic, with a pH level of 5.7. Acid rain is water that has a pH level below 5.7. When lakes are continually replenished with acid rain water, they end up with a pH level that's too low for life in the lake to remain healthy.

Are glaciers and icebergs made of salt water or fresh water?

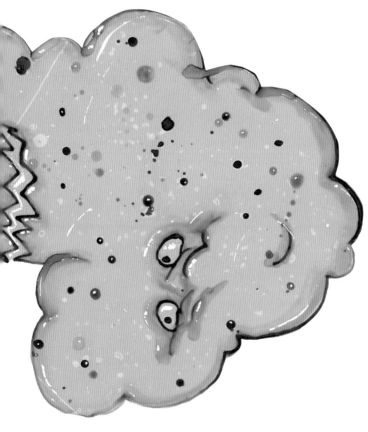

They're both made of fresh water. Glaciers start off as snow. Way up in the mountains, where it's cold all year long, the snow never has a chance to melt. As more and more snow falls, it packs together, squeezing out the air. Eventually huge areas get covered with this thick, heavy ice.

Once these ice fields are about as high as a five-story building, they begin to move, sliding and creeping down the mountain slopes. This moving ice is called a glacier. When glaciers finally meet the sea, huge chunks of ice break off to form floating ice islands—or icebergs. When the chunks of ice break off, the glacier is said to be "calving." Only one-tenth of the iceberg juts out of the water. The rest is hidden below. (Just like an ice cube in a glass of water.) The largest iceberg ever measured was bigger than the country of Belgium!

Scientists think all that frozen fresh water could be useful. They're working on the idea of wrapping huge Antarctic icebergs in plastic insulation to prevent them from melting, and towing them to desert areas. The water could be used for drinking and watering crops.

Can plants protect themselves from being eaten?

You bet. And they have lots of ways to do it. Some have thorns, spines or thistles, others have sword-shaped leaves lined with barbs, some taste awful and others are poisonous.

A rubber tree protects itself with a coating of sticky resin that's like gum. One munch on a rubber tree leaf and the predator gets all gummed up.

The whistling thorn, a type of thorny acacia tree that giraffes love to eat, relies on an ally. At the base of each thorn is a black ball the size of a marble. Ants hollow out the balls and live in them. When a giraffe strips leaves off the whistling thorn tree, the ants pour into the giraffe's nose and bite until it can't stand it any longer and leaves the tree alone. The tree provides a home for the ants and the ants protect the tree from large-scale giraffe attack!

Stinging nettles have little hairs on each leaf. When an animal brushes up against the plant, the tips of these hairs break off and the sap inside is injected into the animal. This sap contains a histamine substance that has the same effect on an animal's skin as a bee sting.

Do plants eat animals?

There are two types of plants that eat animals. One type has moving parts that catch the prey, the other type doesn't.

The Venus flytrap lures insects with its sweet-smelling nectar and a safe-looking landing pad. But insects beware! On this pad are special bristles that are triggered by the insect's arrival. Within a second of an insect landing, the two halves of the leaf close up and the spiny "teeth" on the leaf's edge mesh together. The insect has become dinner. It takes about two weeks for the plant to digest the soft bits. When it's finished, the trap opens again.

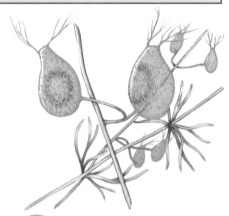

Bladderworts are plants that grow tiny bubble-shaped bladder traps on their stem-like underwater leaves. The bladders have special feeler bristles. When a tiny water animal swims close to the feelers, the bladder snaps open and sucks in the animal.

Sundews have leaves with hairs that produce drops of sticky, slimy, sweet-smelling glue. The insect, attracted by the scent, lands on the leaf and gets stuck. All the hairs then bend over, so that the insect gets covered with slime and eventually suffocates.

Pitcher plants grow in South American and Asian rain forests and in North American bogs. Because the soil is so poor, they need to get extra nourishment from insects. To catch the insects, these bright-colored plants have "pitchers" on the ends of their leaves. The pitchers can be up to 35 cm (14 in) deep and hold as much as a cupful of liquid. Pitcher plants attract insects with sweet-smelling nectar. When an insect lands on the pitcher's slippery rim, it falls in and drowns. The liquid breaks down the insect so the plant can absorb the nutrients it needs.

Deep in the Costa Rican rain forest is a special cousin of the pineapple plant called a **tank bromeliad**. Its huge clump of spiky leaves are joined at the base to catch and hold rain water. In the bromeliad's base it's like a miniature pond, complete with wiggling mosquito larvae, snails and even tadpoles. These little animals mix with decaying plant debris to make up a nutritious soup that feeds the bromeliad.

Why does gum get hard after you've chewed it?

Ever run your hand under a chair and suddenly felt a glob of someone else's old gum? It's disgusting —and it's hard as a rock because the ingredients that made it soft are long gone. These softeners keep the gum pliable by helping it hold in moisture. But as you chew the gum, you chew the softeners out of it. When you finally take it out of your mouth, the moisture evaporates because there aren't any softeners left to hold on to it.

How does an eraser work?

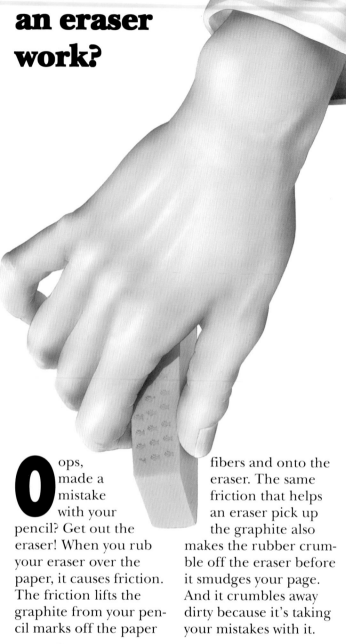

Oops, made a mistake with your pencil? Get out the eraser! When you rub your eraser over the paper, it causes friction. The friction lifts the graphite from your pencil marks off the paper fibers and onto the eraser. The same friction that helps an eraser pick up the graphite also makes the rubber crumble off the eraser before it smudges your page. And it crumbles away dirty because it's taking your mistakes with it.

Are you safe in a car during a lightning storm?

The safest place to be during a lightning storm is inside a building—but stay away from good conductors of electricity, such as TVs, telephones and sinks of water. If you're outside and nowhere near a building, then the next best place to take shelter is in a car. Just make sure it's parked away from telephone poles, trees, high points of ground and large bodies of water because these are the things that are likely to be hit. If something nearby is hit by lightning, the electrical charge from it will travel through the ground. But it won't be able to pass through the rubber tires and into the car.

How long does it take to turn coal into a diamond?

Believe it or not, very few diamonds have ever been made from coal. Most are made from carbon that's found deep in the earth's crust. It can take millions of years for diamonds to form naturally. Why? Carbon requires lots of heat and pressure over many years to drive out all the impurities and rearrange its molecules into a diamond formation. But scientists have figured out a way to speed up the process. By using pure carbon and the right combination of heat and pressure, they can make diamonds in just a few days! These diamonds are very expensive to make, but they're so tough they are used in drills that can slice up concrete. And that's not all. Recently scientists discovered that diamonds can be melted into a very thin but incredibly tough film. When that film is used to coat eyeglasses, for example, it prevents them from becoming scratched.

Where does lint come from?

You pull your clothes out of the clothes dryer and—oh no! They're covered with lint again. As fabric rubs against other fabric, surface fibers loosen, get tangled with other fibers and form lint. Some experts think you might find more lint from blue clothing because blue dyes are harder on fabrics and so the fibers break down and separate more quickly.

Why is it when you're younger you snore less than when you're older?

It's true—it's usually adults who snore. As you get older, your muscles, even those in your mouth and throat, often become looser. When you breathe in while you're sleeping, these muscles and other soft parts inside your mouth and throat are likely to rattle and flap.

And that's what makes that snoring sound. There are other reasons for snoring too: being overweight and even sleeping on your back may cause you to snore. And watch out if you have enlarged tonsils! The air you breathe in when you are sleeping can cause them to rattle and flap, no matter how old you are!

Why does my voice sound funny on a tape recorder?

Although your "tape recorder voice" may sound funny to you, it's close to the way you sound to other people. Why? Normally you hear your voice after it's traveled through the bones in your head. But when you listen to your voice on a tape recorder, you're hearing it after it has traveled through the air. And that makes it sound slightly higher pitched and less muffled than you're used to hearing it.

Is it pitch black inside our bodies?

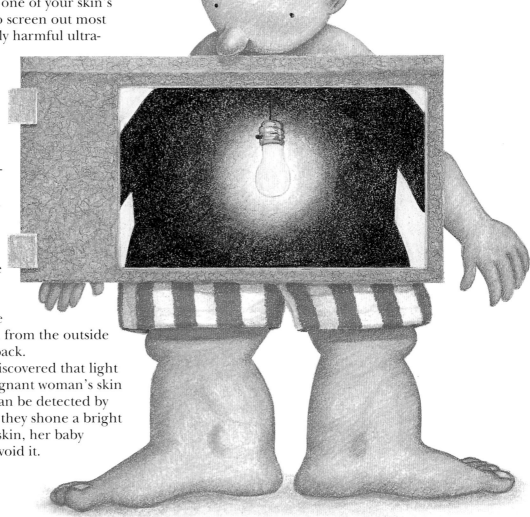

Way down deep it probably is pitch black. In fact, one of your skin's main jobs is to screen out most light, especially harmful ultra-violet rays from the sun. But even though your skin does its job well, some light does get into your body, although not very far. If you have light, untanned skin, you can see this for your-self. Hold your hand up in front of a bright light. You can probably see blue veins close to the surface. Sometimes you can even see a silhouette of the bones in your fin-gers. For you to be able to see blue veins or bone shapes, light has gone in from the outside and has been reflected back.

Recently, scientists discovered that light can travel through a pregnant woman's skin into her belly, where it can be detected by her unborn baby. When they shone a bright light onto the mother's skin, her baby moved or curled up to avoid it.

Why does swimming turn hair green?

If you're blond and you spend a lot of time in a swimming pool that isn't well balanced chemically, go look at your hair. Is it green? If so, blame the chemicals that keep pools clean and clear. These chemicals include copper and chlorine, which com-bine to form tiny green crystals that stick to your hair. If you don't rinse your hair after each dip in the pool, these crystals build up. It happens to every-one's hair, but only blond hair is light enough that it shows. As well, blue coloring in the chlorine makes the yellow of blond hair look even greener. To get rid of the green, use anti-chlorine sham-poo. And ask the own-er of the pool to check its chemical balance.

Why do horses need their hooves trimmed?

Think about what would happen if you didn't cut your fingernails. They would grow longer and longer, start to split and break and eventually curl around if they became long enough. The same thing can happen to a horse's hooves unless they are trimmed every 6 to 12 weeks. Fortunately, getting a hoof trim is no more painful than having a fingernail cut. But it is important. A horse can go lame if it has to walk on chipped or cracked hooves. How do horses out in the wild get their hooves trimmed? They don't. The hard ground they run around on wears down their hooves naturally.

Do hamsters ever get paper cuts when they gnaw on paper?

Like all rodents, a hamster has teeth that grow continuously during its lifetime. To prevent them from growing too long, a hamster will wear down its teeth by gnawing on seeds, paper and twigs. Most of the time it does this without cutting itself. And if it does get a paper cut, chances are the cut will heal on its own. Sometimes, though, a paper cut can cause problems. Your hamster's mouth may become so sore that it stops eating and drinking. If that happens, take your pet to the vet so the cut can be cleaned. You can avoid the problem by giving your hamster tissue or paper towels to use for its nest.

Why do my cat's eyes change shape?

Next time you're in a dimly lit room with your cat, look closely at its eyes. The pupils will be round and big. But if you switch on a bright light, they'll shrink to narrow slits. In a similar way your pupils shrink down to tiny circles in bright light. But unlike you, cats are night hunters. They need to be able to see well in the dark. So their pupils open up exceptionally wide to let in as much light as possible. That's probably why you notice the change so much.

What kind of pig is a guinea pig?

When is a pig not a pig? When it's a guinea pig! Guinea pigs, along with hamsters and gerbils, belong to the rodent family. Pigs, on the other hand, are part of the swine family. No one knows for sure how this South American rodent got its name. It probably has to do with the squeals and grunts that a guinea pig makes—especially while eating.

Why are a rabbit's ears colder than its body?

A rabbit's body acts the same way your body does when it gets cold. It pumps most of its blood to its internal organs to keep them warm and away from other less important places, including its ears. Because those areas receive less blood, they feel cold. Even in warm weather a rabbit's ears are cool. Why? The hot rabbit's body sends warmed-up blood to its ears. There, the heat from the blood is transferred into the cooler air around the ears. The large surface area of the rabbit's ears, along with their thin skin, help the heat to escape. Then the blood flows back to the body to cool the rabbit.

Where are a budgie's ears?

It's difficult to see a budgie's ears because they have no external parts like people's do —but they're certainly there. Look for a round patch of feathers on each side of its head. These feathers cover and protect a small opening about the size of a crayon tip. That's the budgie's ear. How well can a budgie hear? Quite well—even with feathers covering the ear! A budgie relies on its hearing to keep near the flock. If one budgie can't hear the calls of another, it knows it's straying too far. A budgie's keen sense of hearing also helps it learn to imitate words.

Why does an elephant have such big ears?

An elephant's extra-large ears help it keep cool. Those big ears are full of blood vessels that act like radiators. When the elephant gets too hot, it just flaps its ears to let out the heat. There's another reason those big ears come in handy. When spread wide, an elephant's ears make it look even more huge and threatening to its enemies.

Does a ride in an elevator make my dog's ears pop?

You might be surprised to hear that you and your dog have similar kinds of ears. So if your ears are popping as the air pressure changes in a moving elevator, your dog's ears are probably popping too. When that happens, your dog may open and close its mouth several times to gulp air. Or it may even yawn. But your pet's not bored or tired. Just like you, it's trying to avoid that uncomfortable ear popping!

Why do dogs gobble their food?

When Fido gobbles his food without pausing for breath, he's probably only doing what comes naturally. Long ago before dogs lived with people, they lived in groups called wild packs. When a kill was made, the leaders of the pack ate first. Then the rest of the pack got whatever was left. Any dog that didn't eat fast didn't eat at all!

Why are dalmatians always pictured on fire trucks?

Back in the days when fire trucks were pulled by horses, dalmatians were a fire fighter's best friend. The dalmatians ran beside the trucks and prevented other dogs from coming up and biting at the horses' heels. When they reached the fire, the dogs would guard the equipment and keep the horses still. Their speedy running and ability to get along with horses made dalmatians perfect for this job—until motorized fire trucks came along and dogs were no longer needed. At some fire stations, these dogs are still kept as mascots or good luck symbols. And the fire fighters have discovered something else about dalmatians. With their keen sense of smell, dalmatians can sniff out dangerous liquids that might catch fire and explode. Doggone it!

Why does a pointer point?

Pointing comes naturally to a pointer. Scientists believe that the pointing instinct began with the pointer's relative, the wolf. When a wolf smells prey, it freezes and points itself in the direction of the scent. Pointers have been bred to develop this pointing instinct. But they also need training. When well instructed, they're almost always accurate at picking up the direction of the scent.

How do guide dogs know when it's safe to cross the road?

Not by looking at the traffic lights, that's for sure. Why? All dogs are color-blind. They can't tell green from red. Instead, a guide dog counts on its owner. It's the owner who knows when to cross the road by listening to the direction of the traffic flow. But if it's unsafe, the dog will refuse to cross. That's because the dog is trained to disobey an owner's command if it threatens the person's safety. This is called "intelligent disobedience." A guide dog takes its job very seriously. As soon as it begins its training, it learns that being in a harness means being "on the job." So if you see a guide dog at work, be careful not to distract it by petting or feeding it.

Do dogs have belly buttons?

Yes, dogs, like all mammals, have belly buttons— but they are not easy to see. Unlike your belly button, your dog's is small and almost flat —just a bit of scar tissue hidden by fur. Vets are usually the only people who see them, when they shave a dog's stomach before surgery. A dog's belly button is located just about where yours is—in the middle of the tummy.

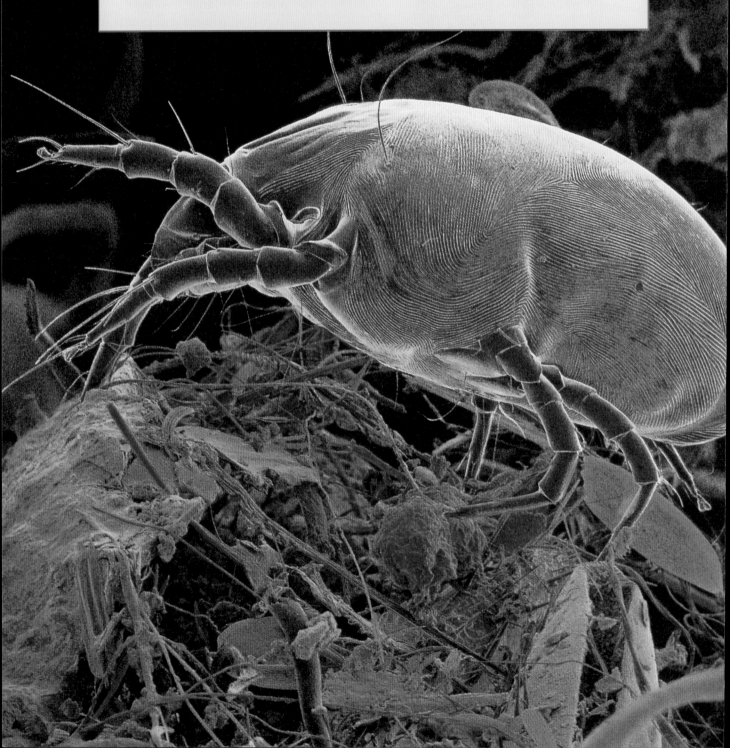

What's the smallest living thing in the world?

What's your guess? A flea? Well, it's pretty small. In fact it's about the size of this ✦. But dust mites are even smaller. Bacteria are even smaller than dust mites and viruses are even smaller than bacteria! This world is full of things so small they are scarcely imaginable . . . and guess where many of them live. In your room!

Dust Mites

Your house, no matter how clean, is filled with dust mites (left). They are chubby little things with eight legs that live in carpets and beds. They munch their way through—are you ready for this?—flakes of human skin. You shed thousands of skin flakes every minute, and these busy mites help clean your room by gobbling them up. But dust mites might not be completely helpful. If you're allergic to house dust, it may be the dust mite droppings in it that are causing you problems.

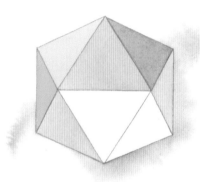

Cold Viruses

Probably the very smallest living thing is a virus. If anyone in your house has a cold, there will be cold viruses everywhere. They are so small that you could line up half a million of them across your little fingernail! Some scientists think you pick up cold viruses by touching an object that's just been touched by an infected person. Then when you touch your nose or eyes, bingo! You're soon sneezing. Other scientists think you get the virus from the air. If someone sneezes, cold viruses are shot into the air at up to 65 km/h (42 mph) and they can float there for hours. If you've got a cold, blow your nose carefully. Tissues are full of holes and you don't want to spread your virus around.

Fleas

If you have a pet, you probably know all about fleas. They, or their eggs or larvae, hide in the carpet. It's not much fun to get bitten by one, but fleas are interesting creatures if you get down to their level. For one thing, they're great jumpers. When a flea's leg muscles get moving, the flea can shoot through the air 250 times as far as its length with its long legs flailing around wildly. If the flea is lucky, those hairy legs will latch on to your pet's fur. If *you* are lucky, they won't latch on to you.

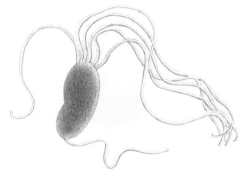

Bacteria

Bacteria cover everything, but they like to settle on your face in particular. It's warm and damp and provides plenty of good food. There's salt water from perspiration, a little oil, some proteins from your skin . . . no wonder it's such a popular place. What kind of bacteria like your face? Some come in clusters like bunches of grapes. Others lie around like strings of sausages. And there are even bacteria that spin a "propeller" to move.

Eyelash Mites

These harmless sausage-shaped creatures snuggle down among the roots of your eyelashes. Eyelash mites feed on oil and other secretions at the base of your lashes, helping to keep the area clean. Occasionally one will climb up to the surface of your skin at night and move on to another eyelash. But don't wait up with a flashlight, hoping to catch one. They're much too tiny to see!

WACKY WILDLIFE QUIZ

1. Camels have:
a) bald heads
b) webbed feet
c) 15 toes on each foot

2. A crayfish has:
a) two eyes in its head
b) three eyes—two in its head, one in its tail
c) four eyes—two in its head, two on its antennae

3. The horns of the great horned owl:
a) go limp when it rains
b) are made of feathers
c) get caught in trees

4. Kangaroos that have front legs as long as their back legs:
a) live in trees
b) live in Spain
c) live in condominiums

5. A cross section of a hummingbird's tongue looks like:
a) a U
b) a V
c) a W

6. Snakes, like people, can:
a) yodel
b) giggle
c) yawn

7. A spider's blood, when exposed to oxygen, turns:
a) invisible
b) upside down
c) blue

8. The wood turtle catches worms by:
a) stamping its feet on the ground to make them curious
b) using perfume to attract them
c) leaping on them from high branches

9. A snake stays clean because:
a) dirt doesn't stick to its smooth skin
b) it sheds its skin whenever it gets dirty
c) it never plays in the dirt

10. When a turtle retreats into its shell, its neck:
a) folds up like an accordion
b) folds into an S shape
c) folds up like a telescope

11. Snow monkeys survive the Japanese winters by:
a) flying to Hawaii
b) drinking lots of hot tea
c) soaking in hot springs

12. When a tadpole turns into a frog, its tail:
a) gets used up as food by its body
b) turns curly
c) drops off

13. The blue whale is so big:
a) an oil tanker could sail into its mouth
b) its tail flaps cause tidal waves
c) its tongue can weigh more than an elephant

14. Most turtles are:
a) pink with purple spots
b) blind
c) deaf

15. Bats "walk" on their:
a) feet
b) knuckles
c) elbows

16. When penguins moult, they're not heavy enough to dive for food, so they:
a) pull themselves down along seaweed stems
b) swallow pebbles to add weight
c) visit the nearest dive-in restaurant

17. A startled kangaroo will:
a) cry
b) cough
c) burst into song

18. An elephant looks behind itself by:
a) turning its body
b) looking between its legs
c) looking in a rearview mirror

Why does an elephant have tusks and a trunk?

An elephant uses its trunk and tusks for very specific purposes. Its tusks are its most visible teeth. Permanent tusks appear when the elephant is two to three years old and continue growing all its life. An elephant uses its tusks as crowbars for peeling bark off trees, as fork-lifts for moving obstacles and as pickaxes for digging holes. They are also deadly weapons. But more importantly, perhaps, elephants help each other dig deep wells with their tusks. During droughts these wells are vital to the survival of many animals, not just the elephants who dig them.

An elephant's trunk is really just a multi-purpose nose. The elephant breathes through it and also uses it to sniff out danger, even from far away. The trunk has other uses too. It acts like a strong and agile hand, capable of picking up anything from tree trunks to peanuts. And it's like a vacuum cleaner. It can suck up enough water at one time to fill eight 2-L (2-qt) milk cartons.

How much does an elephant eat?

During the 16 hours each day that it spends eating, a large bull elephant can eat the equivalent of 2,300 hamburgers in vegetation and wash it down with enough water to fill 608 milkshake cups.

24

Is it true that elephants never forget?

There's no question that elephants have powerful brains. One elephant was taught to run an automatic feeding machine after she heard a certain series of notes. The elephant was able to do it even if the notes were played with other notes or played on different instruments. After a year and a half of not being tested, the elephant was still able to remember most of the notes she had learned. Another elephant spent a lot of time with two scientists who taught her to match up picture puzzles. She was able to do the test almost perfectly after a year. Then the scientists went away and didn't see her for 32 years. When they returned, she obviously remembered them. She even hugged them with her trunk! But she didn't do very well on the matching game. And then there's the story of an elephant who, as a reward, was given a pebble by a worker instead of the usual lump of cane sugar. Five weeks later, when the elephant met up with the man, it reached into its cheek pocket, pulled out the pebble and threw it at him. So what does all this mean? Probably that elephants remember things that are useful for them to know—like how to get food. And that some elephants remember things better than others, just like people.

How do I remember things?

When you want to remember things you tap into your seahorse and walnut. Without them you wouldn't be able to remember much at all. It's not as crazy as it sounds. The seahorse is a part of your brain that you need to file away new memories. It's called the hippocampus and, yes, it's shaped like a seahorse. Without your hippocampus, you could read this page again and again and never remember it.

The walnut is the place in your brain where different kinds of memories are matched up. Its scientific name is the amygdala, which describes its nut-like shape. When you answer the telephone and hear your friend's voice, you'll immediately picture her face. That's because your amygdala links up your memory of her voice with the memory of her face. It happens so quickly, you don't even think about doing it!

Why can't I remember what it was like to be a baby?

Most people can't remember things that happened before they were three or four years old. Scientists aren't sure why, but one theory is it's because the brain you had as a baby and the one you have now are like two different computers that store memories different ways. When you upgraded to a new computer, you could no longer retrieve the files stored in your old one.

What's the difference between short-term and long-term memory?

They are different kinds of memory. Short-term memory is what you use when you're dialing a telephone number you have just learned. You will remember it long enough to dial it, but unless that number is important to you, you will soon forget it. And it's short-term memory you use to cram for a test. You may know everything for the test, but a week later most of the facts will probably be history.

The other kind of memory you have is long-term memory. Long-term memories are the ones you can remember years after they've happened. Not everything makes it into your long-term memory because it takes a few minutes for a memory to get there. But once it's there, you will be able to remember that memory again and again.

Sometimes a particular event is so special or shocking that when you recall it, you will remember not only the event itself but where you were and who you were with when it happened. This is called a flashbulb memory.

What happens if you don't have a memory?

You know what it's like to forget something—but imagine what it would be like not to remember anything at all. There is a man who stopped remembering after his hippocampus was disconnected during a brain operation 40 years ago. He can remember things from before the operation—but nothing that has happened since then. If you met him yesterday and then again today, he wouldn't recognize you. He gets upset every time he hears of his favorite uncle's death, even though it happened years ago. He never remembers being told about it—no matter how many times people break the sad news to him.

27

What is a seahorse?

Believe it or not, a seahorse is a fish, found in shallow ocean waters all around the world. A seahorse is related to pipe fish and sea-dragons. Both seahorses and sea-dragons feature impressive body armor and a sucking snout. But only the seahorse can change color to match its surroundings. This camouflage comes in handy when the seahorse is trying to catch its dinner or hide from predators.

Why does a seahorse have a tail?

The seahorse's tail, like a monkey's, is prehensile, which means it's made for grasping. A newborn seahorse uses its tail to hang on tight to a brother, sister or whatever's handy while it gets its bearings. When danger or dinner approaches, a seahorse wraps its tail around a seaweed stem, sways with the current and waits for the enemy to pass . . . or the tasty crustacean to come close enough to be slurped up. When a male and a female perform their courtship dance, they wrap their tails around the same object and circle it like perfectly matched dancers.

How does a seahorse swim?

A seahorse usually swims upright in a slow and unfish-like manner. But don't be fooled. Living full-time under-water, the seahorse has to be a good swimmer. To move forward, it flaps its dorsal fin 35 beats per second and uses its head and fins to steer.

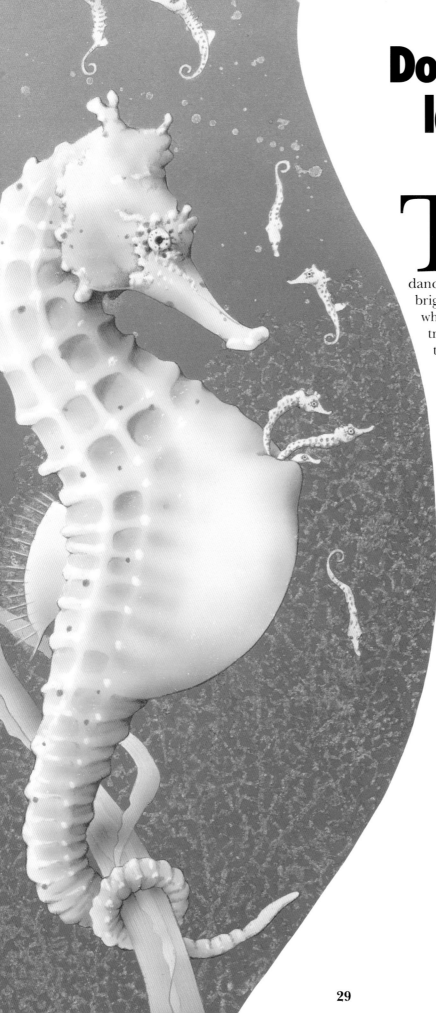

Do seahorses lay eggs?

The female does, but it's the father who has the babies. Sound strange? Here's how it works. First the seahorses spend several days "courting"—they dance together in circles and their colors brighten. After three days of courtship, when the female's eggs are ripe, she transfers them to the male's pouch through a long, thin tube called an ovipositor. The eggs are then fertilized and become embedded in the pouch wall, where the male's blood vessels supply them with oxygen and nourishment. During the two to seven weeks of pregnancy, the fluid in the father's sealed pouch becomes more and more like sea water so the newborns will be used to the ocean's saltiness when they're born.

Having babies is hard work—especially when you have several hundred! Pumping them out of his pouch usually takes the father days. Although less than 12 mm (½ in) long, the baby is totally independent—swimming, feeding and trying out its tail. At one year, it's full grown—up to 34 cm (14 in) long for some seahorses—and ready for kids of its own.

Can animals smell better than we can?

Some animals can and it's a good thing too. Why? They rely on their super sniffers to find food and avoid danger.

Long Noses

An elephant has a longer nose than any other animal. So it probably won't surprise you to learn that it's very useful. When an elephant sticks its trunk straight up in the air, it can smell danger up to 5 km (3 mi) away! And with its long snout, an anteater (below) can smell 40 times better than we can. That comes in handy when you're sniffing out something as small as an ant.

Swimming Nose

A shark usually hunts down the squid and fish that it eats. But competition for food in the ocean is fierce, so sometimes a shark counts on its super sense of smell to find other animals' prey. In a strong current, it can smell blood from over 1.6 km (1 mi) away. No wonder the shark is nicknamed "the swimming nose."

Follow Your Nose

The star-nosed mole not only smells with its nose, it "sees" with it too. The tentacles circling its nostrils are super-sensitive—almost like 22 wriggling fingers on a round pink hand. Whether it's scurrying through dark tunnels or swimming in murky water, they help the nearly blind mole learn about its surroundings and pick out its favorite foods—insects, worms and leeches—better than eyes ever could.

Flying Noses

Some high flyers rely on their noses too. Turkey vultures, flying over dense forests, use their nifty noses to sniff out carcasses lying hidden below the trees on the forest floor. One whiff of a possible meal and these birds take a nose-dive!

How do sea turtles find their way back to the beach where they were born?

The minute green sea turtles hatch out of their eggs they scamper down the beach and head out to sea. There they'll spend most of their lives. But, as many as 50 years after her birth, a female sea turtle braves a long and difficult trip to come back to the very same beach to lay her eggs. This is only one of several return trips she makes. How does she find her way home? No one really knows for sure, but the latest theory is that when she's far out at sea she navigates by the stars and the moon. Then, when she gets closer to home, she sniffs out the water currents until she detects the smell of her home sand. Navigating by that smell and by local landmarks, such as large rocks that jut out into the water, she follows her nose . . . all the way home.

What happens to our garbage?

That depends on how you throw it out. If you have a compost heap, you know that organic garbage—like carrot peels, orange rinds and salad leftovers—can be piled up in a compost and left to decompose. The result? Great fertilizer.

But what about all the stuff you load into bags and leave out for the garbage collectors? It gets tossed into their truck, compacted and carted off either to a huge incinerator, where it is burned, or to a landfill site.

What is a landfill site?

A landfill site is a huge dump that's specially built to hold your garbage. First a deep, wide hole is dug. Then it's lined with thick plastic to try to stop toxic chemicals—found in household cleaners and industrial wastes—from seeping into the ground. Once the site is ready, trucks bring in their loads of garbage and dump them. Huge tractors spread the garbage around and cover each layer with dirt. The layers of garbage and dirt are piled up until the pit is filled. Then it's time to look for a new dump site. Almost 80 percent of our garbage ends up in landfills. As the human population increases, landfill sites are filling up quickly. So we need to reduce the amount of garbage by avoiding over-packaged foods and buying in bulk, as well as by recycling and reusing.

What happens to the things that are recycled?

How would you feel about wearing a pop bottle, putting all your trash in a milk jug or driving on crushed glass? Don't laugh. Chances are you have done all these things!

At the moment about 10 percent of our garbage is recycled. Check out these new looks. Grass, leaves and kitchen scraps are chopped up and mixed with other organic garbage to make fertilizer. Used paper and cardboard is turned back into pulp, which is used to make new paper. Old glass bottles are crushed into pieces and melted down to make new glass or transformed into glasphalt for roads. Aluminum cans are melted down into sheets of aluminum and shaped into new cans. Plastic milk jugs are used to make trash cans and flowerpots. Plastic soft drink bottles are ground into flakes and used as pellets for filling in parkas and sleeping bags. Or these soft drink bottles, along with bottled water containers, are turned into car bumpers. Used tires are turned into flooring and rubber mats. And old cars are crushed and melted and the resulting steel is made into new cars.

What does biodegradable mean?

If something is biodegradable it can be broken down naturally by micro-organisms in the soil, water or sewage. It's nature's way of cleaning up. Some things—like leaves or paper—biodegrade quickly. Other things—like most plastics—take centuries to decompose. Nature can't keep up with all that we're throwing out. So we need to help. One way we can help is to use "biodegradable" and phosphate-free cleaning products—such as soaps and detergents—which break down quickly and don't contain toxic chemicals that pollute.

What exactly is the greenhouse effect?

The greenhouse effect is nothing new. It's caused by gases in the earth's atmosphere. Some of these gases—such as carbon dioxide and methane—have always been around, helping to keep our planet warm enough for people, plants and animals to survive. But now the greenhouse gases are increasing. Scientists worry about the effect that this will have on the temperature of Earth's surface. Here's why.

If you've ever been in a greenhouse, you know how hot it can get. Sunlight streams through the glass and heats up the plants. Then the heat radiates back out from the plants and is trapped by the greenhouse walls and roof, keeping it warmer inside than outside.

Earth gets warmed up in the same kind of way. Sunlight passes through Earth's atmosphere to reach the surface and warm it up. The heat then radiates back up into the atmosphere. Because of the greenhouse gases, some of that radiated heat is trapped. The rest escapes out into space.

Until now there has been a balance between the heat coming down from the sun and that bouncing back into space. Now, this denser layer of gases acts like a double window to keep in the heat. More of these heat rays are trapped by this extra layer and bounced back to Earth again, instead of escaping out into space. Those trapped rays mean more heat to warm up Earth's surface. And that's what's known as "the greenhouse effect."

Why is the greenhouse effect increasing?

It's increasing because more and more greenhouse gases, carbon dioxide and methane, are being spewed into the air. Much of this is because of things people do. Every time we burn coal, oil and gas, we release carbon dioxide into the atmosphere. The more carbon dioxide there is, the more the atmosphere acts like a greenhouse roof. But it's not only that we produce carbon dioxide. Whenever we cut down trees and plants we destroy the very things that take carbon dioxide out of the air. Every tree gobbles up about 20 kg (44 lb) of carbon dioxide each year and breathes out oxygen. And when we burn areas of rain forest we also send into the atmosphere tremendous amounts of carbon dioxide stored in those trees.

But people aren't the only ones to blame. There are two "natural" greenhouse gas culprits:

termites and cows! When termites eat, their metabolic process releases huge amounts of carbon dioxide and methane into the atmosphere. You might not think that the tiny termite could have much effect, but there are around 250,000 billion termites in the world. And although there are a mere 1.3 billion cattle on Earth, they are said to be responsible for pumping 100 million tonnes (tons) of methane into the atmosphere annually. That's a LOT of gas!

What does it matter if the earth gets a bit warmer?

I f the earth gets warmer, scientists think there will be an increase in the number of droughts and tropical storms. The oceans will rise and coastal cities could be flooded, because the polar ice caps will start to melt. Warmer temperatures will turn some fertile land into desert and will also heat up the oceans, causing the death of many fragile sea plants and animals. Today, people everywhere are working together to burn less fuel and pump less carbon dioxide into the air. And you can help. Walk or ride your bike instead of asking your parents to drive you places. They'll save gas, too.

How much milk does a cow give in a day?

Some cows are better at making milk than others. The Holstein, below, is one breed of cow that is known for the high amount of milk it gives. In a single day, a healthy Holstein might produce about 100 glasses of milk!

How quickly can a cow turn hay into milk?

Believe it or not, it can happen in just 24 hours. Here's how it works. Unlike your stomach, a cow's stomach has four chambers, or sections. When a cow swallows a mouthful of partly chewed corn, wheat, barley or hay it goes into the first chamber, called the rumen. Here, bacteria and other tiny one-celled animals called protozoans help break down the food into materials the cow's stomach can

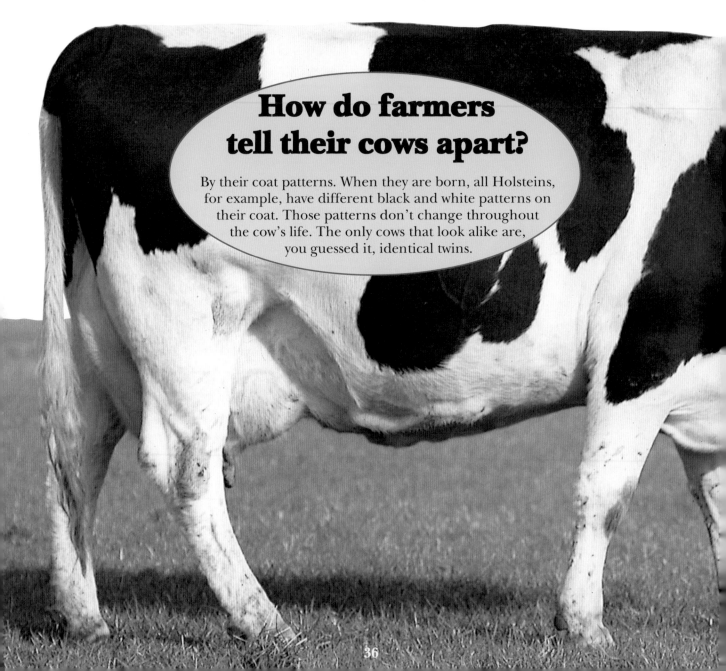

How do farmers tell their cows apart?

By their coat patterns. When they are born, all Holsteins, for example, have different black and white patterns on their coat. Those patterns don't change throughout the cow's life. The only cows that look alike are, you guessed it, identical twins.

absorb. After a few hours the cow brings this partly digested mash—called cud—back up into her mouth and chews it some more. When she swallows again, the cud goes down into the second, third and fourth chambers and then on into the small intestine where nutrients from the food—vitamins, proteins, fats, minerals, carbohydrates, and water—are absorbed into the blood. The cow's body holds on to the nutrients it needs to stay healthy and strong. The rest are taken to the udder, where they are converted into milk. A full udder can weigh up to 27 kg (60 lb)! When the cow is ready to be milked, a milking machine or a person squeezes the milk out through one or more of the four nipples or teats on the udder.

Can cows jump?

Not over the moon, if that's what you're thinking. But although you won't find them sailing through the sky, they can jump. If they're running fast enough, they can even make it over a low fence.

Is cow manure used for anything?

Many people spread manure on their lawn or garden to improve the soil, but Southern California has come up with a more unlikely use for . . . ahem . . . cow pies. They built the world's first commercial power plant that's fueled entirely by cow manure. The plant buys cow dung from farmers and lets it dry in the sun. Then it's taken into the plant and dried again. The dung becomes so dry it spontaneously combusts. The resulting heat powers a generator that gives light and heat to 20,000 Southern Californian homes. The plant relies on about 250,000 cattle for their, er, output, and uses up about 1000 tonnes (tons) of manure each day! It's a great way to create clean power and solve an existing waste problem.

Why does mozzarella cheese stretch more than cheddar?

When cheddar cheese is made, its curds, or milk solids, are heated and stirred until they harden. This binds all the protein molecules tightly together. If you melt cheddar cheese and try to stretch it, the molecules will break apart. Mozzarella cheese curds are treated differently. While the cheese cooks, its curds are stretched by a machine. This pulling and stretching makes the cheese's protein molecules line up, intead of bunching together. When you pull on melted mozzarella cheese, the molecules stretch apart but remain attached, so the cheese stretches.

What makes milk turn sour?

Most milk turns bad, not sour. What's the difference? Milk used to leave dairies containing fast-growing bacteria. As these bacteria grew, they fed on sugars in the milk and changed them into acids that turned the milk sour so that it tasted like buttermilk. Today, dairies are more sterile and milk no longer contains these speedy bacteria.

But it does contain slower-growing bacteria that love the cold of your refrigerator. If you use up your milk before the date stamped on its container, the milk is safe and healthy to drink. But if you let it sit in your fridge, the slower bacteria have time to break down the milk's proteins and fats and turn the milk bad. And that's a very different taste from sour milk. Yech!

Why don't you get a sunburn when you're sitting in a car?

When you're outside in direct sunlight, ultraviolet (UV) light rays—both A and B—hit your skin. You can't see either kind, but both are damaging. When UV-B light rays shine on you, they damage your skin. To protect you, your skin produces more melanin, the substance that gives you a tan. When you're inside a car, the windows act like a shield. They absorb and block the UV-B rays so you don't get burned. But don't be fooled. Glass lets through ultraviolet-A rays. And they may be just as damaging. They won't burn you, but they will cause the skin to sag and wrinkle and get all leathery.

If movies are made of "still" pictures, why do we see them as "moving"?

Close your eyes for a moment, then open them quickly and close them again. The image of what you saw stays with you for a short time. That's because your retinas, the sensitive screens on the backs of your eyeballs, hang on to what they have seen. When you watch a movie, the same thing happens. Movies are made of still pictures, each slightly different from the next, flashed one after the other on a screen, 24 times a second. But you don't see the pictures individually. Instead, your brain blends them together so that the pictures appear to be continuous and moving.

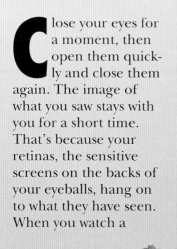

What is the ozone layer?

High up in the atmosphere, about 25 km (16 mi) above Earth, is a layer of bluish-colored ozone gas known as the ozone layer. This is Earth's "good" ozone and it's constantly being created as oxygen reacts with the sun's ultraviolet, or UV, light. This ozone layer is extremely important to Earth. Why? It's a delicate filter that shields us from the sun's harmful UV rays.

What's happening to the ozone layer and why?

Scientists have discovered that the ozone layer is thinning over parts of North America, Europe and Asia and that there are holes over the North and South poles. These holes are caused by artificial chemicals that gobble up ozone faster than it's being made. The biggest chemical culprits are halons and chlorofluorocarbons (CFCs), which are used in some aerosol and foam products and coolants in fridges and air conditioners. At ground level, CFCs are safe and stable. But when products containing CFCs are made, burned or thrown away, CFCs are released into the air, where they are zapped by the sun's UV radiation. This causes them to break down into individual atoms of chlorine, fluorine and carbon, and that's when the real trouble starts. A freed-up chlorine atom can gobble up tens of thousands of ozone molecules before it latches on to something else or floats back down to Earth.

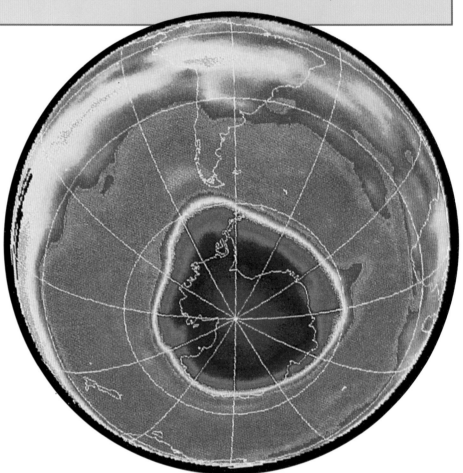

What's "bad" ozone?

Ozone in the earth's upper atmosphere protects us from some of the sun's harmful ultraviolet rays, but ozone down at Earth's surface is a dangerous form of air pollution. This ozone is produced from the reaction between motor vehicle exhausts or factory smoke and sunlight. "Bad" ozone is part of the smog over large cities. The smog is deadly: it's unhealthy for people and plants, destroys buildings and even cracks rubber. That's why people who live in sunny, smoggy places like Los Angeles have to replace their windshield wipers often, even though they're rarely used!

Does ozone have anything to do with the greenhouse effect?

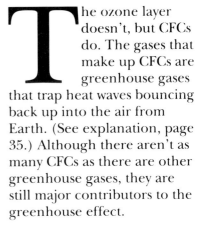

The ozone layer doesn't, but CFCs do. The gases that make up CFCs are greenhouse gases that trap heat waves bouncing back up into the air from Earth. (See explanation, page 35.) Although there aren't as many CFCs as there are other greenhouse gases, they are still major contributors to the greenhouse effect.

Can we fix the holes in the ozone layer?

We can't fix the holes, but we can stop contributing to the problem. To help save the ozone layer, people refused to buy aerosol cans containing CFCs. The can ban worked—today most aerosols in North America don't contain this dangerous chemical. And there's even better news: 90 countries have promised to ban CFCs completely by the year 2000. You can help protect the ozone layer by using products that are labeled "CFC free." If we stop sending CFCs up into the air, the holes will eventually fix themselves naturally.

How do animals keep cool in the heat?

Other Side, Please!

Fritillary butterflies enjoy the sunlight—but sometimes it's too strong for them. To beat the heat, these butterflies often head for the shade. If they can't find shade, they simply fold up their wings and turn their back on the sun. Or they may face the sun directly. Because they're exposing less of their body and wings to the sun, they absorb less heat—and stay cooler.

Take a Nap

Small enough to hold in your hand, the desert jerboa avoids the sun's hot rays by sleeping in an underground burrow during the day. It plugs up the entrance so that moist, cool air stays inside. At night when things cool down, the jerboa emerges to search for food. If it's still warm, the jerboa counts on its large, thin-skinned ears to keep it cool by channeling excess heat away from its body.

Get in a Flap

The flying fox, or fruit bat, sleeps in the trees on warm days, usually in shady, breezy spots. But when the temperature rises, the flying fox may get in a flap—to keep cool! This bat has been spotted stretching out a wing and waving it back and forth just the way you'd use a fan.

Time for a Dip

When things really warm up, there's nothing more refreshing than taking a dip. And that's exactly what the common skink does—only it goes for a "swim" in the sand! The skink, a reptile, lives in the deserts of Africa where there's very little water. But that doesn't stop it from taking a cooling swim. Sinking just below the surface of the sand, the skink folds its legs against its body and slowly glides forward in a snake-like way. The skink skims along in search of beetles and millipedes, nicely protected from the sun.

Kangaroo Cool Down

Ever heard of licking the heat—with your tongue? Well, meet a hot kangaroo. First, instead of sweating, like horses and people do, the kangaroo licks its arms and legs over and under. The moisture evaporates, causing the blood vessels just beneath the skin to cool down. Then the cooler blood circulates throughout the kangaroo's body, helping to lower its temperature. Now that's a cool kangaroo!

How do trees protect themselves from bad weather?

It's cold and rainy, you can't go anywhere warm and dry, and you don't have an umbrella. Sounds bleak? Not if you're a tree. Trees are built to withstand the weather in their area. For example, some trees—such as red and silver maples, and poplars—try to minimize rain damage by turning up their leaves when rain threatens. That way the leaves won't get ripped off or broken by the rain bursting through them.

But it's not just rain that causes problems: blowing winds, snow and strong sun can be equally tough on even the tallest trees. Willows are well adapted for windy climates. Their flexible trunks and branches won't snap and their narrow leaves won't get whipped around by strong winds. Douglas fir trees that grow in high snowfall areas have very droopy branches. When snow falls it just slides right off. If the branches were flat and rigid they would snap under the weight of the snow. Other alpine trees avoid snow damage by being so skinny that very little snow actually lands on them. To beat the heat, palo verde trees grow leaves when it rains and drop them when the weather turns dry and hot.

What's the oldest a tree can grow?

Have you ever heard the song "Tie a yellow ribbon 'round the old oak tree"? Well, it's true. Oak trees do grow old, up to almost 1,200 years old, in fact. But they aren't the champs. Neither are the 2,000- year-old yew trees in England. These are just young things when compared with bristlecone pines that grow in the mountains of the American Southwest. Bristlecones can reach the extraordinary age of more than 4,000 years old! What's their secret? They're built to withstand the toughest conditions imaginable—even poor soil, little water and constant winds don't defeat them. Why? Bristlecones don't grow very tall—only 5 to 12 m (16 to 40 ft), and they have a high resin content that protects the wood from moisture and rot.

How do trees and plants clean the air?

What's clear-cut logging?

Clear-cut logging means cutting down all the big trees in an area. Sometimes it's the best way to log an area, if a forest fire has raged through it, or if the area to be logged is small. But it's not always a good way to log for two reasons. Once all the big trees are gone, there is little to keep the soil from washing away in the rain or blowing away in the wind. Also, there's nothing to protect delicate young trees from the weather. To avoid these problems, smart forest companies rely on "selective logging." This means they cut down some trees and leave others to protect the soil and the young seedlings.

Trees and plants are our major allies in the fight against pollution. Why? They breathe in carbon dioxide that's spewed into the air in car exhaust and factory smoke. And they breathe out the oxygen that people and animals need to live.

In the past few decades, we've been pumping more and more carbon dioxide into our atmosphere by burning coal, oil and gas. At the same time, we've been cutting down the trees and plants that convert the carbon dioxide in the atmosphere into oxygen. In order to keep the atmosphere balanced, we need to burn fewer fossil fuels in our cars, factories and homes and find alternative sources of energy. We also need to plant more trees and be very careful about how we log our forests.

Why aren't forests filled with dead wood?

◆

Recycling is nothing new to Mother Nature. She has a whole crew of creatures devoted to doing just that. These recycling pros are constantly at work, cleaning up the old dead wood that litters the forest floor.

Compost Gardening

Huge colonies of atta leaf-cutting ants (left), which live in tropical and subtropical America, help out by compost gardening. The ants set up a certain type of fungus garden. Then they cut up and carry home leaves and flowers from several types of plants and feed it to the fungus. The fungi are crucial to the forest recycling process because they break down the tough, woody plant stems. When the ants get hungry, or need food for their brood, they eat the fungus. Leaf cutters and fungus make great recycling allies!

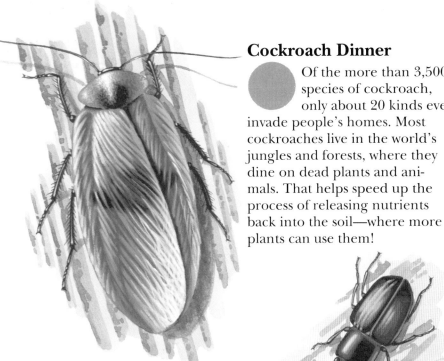

Cockroach Dinner

Of the more than 3,500 species of cockroach, only about 20 kinds ever invade people's homes. Most cockroaches live in the world's jungles and forests, where they dine on dead plants and animals. That helps speed up the process of releasing nutrients back into the soil—where more plants can use them!

Tunneling Beetles

There are several beetles that wolf down wood. Bark beetles group together on old or fallen trees. They burrow into the tree and make "galleries" or tunnels as they eat their way up its length. Special bacteria in their intestines help break down the wood so the beetles can digest it.

Termite Treats

Imagine eating the chair you're sitting on or the book you're reading. Wood and paper are meat and potatoes to a termite. So are cotton and cardboard. These strange tastes make termites dangerous houseguests; they can literally eat your house out from under you. But termites are handy to have around in a forest. Thanks to their taste for wood, especially soft, moist wood, they break down dead trees and help keep the forest floor uncluttered.

How much wood can a woodchuck chuck?

Believe it or not, none! "Woodchuck" is just another name for a groundhog, the rodent that's famous for its February 2nd weather report. It is said that if it sees its shadow when it pops out of its burrow, the groundhog scurries back in. And that means there's another six weeks of winter ahead. Once it does stop hibernating, the groundhog comes up to feast on grass, leaves, flowers and the odd insect. The closest it gets to "chucking wood" is when it nibbles on tree bark. So while a woodchuck may be able to chuck wood, it hasn't the least interest in doing so.

What's the difference between rain forests and other forests?

The difference has to do with the high humidity and the large amount of rain (at least 250 cm/100 in) that falls throughout the year. Most rain forests are found near the equator in the tropics, where the climate is hot and rainy. There's one other difference. When large areas of tropical rain forests are cleared, the forests don't have the same ability to regenerate themselves that other forests do.

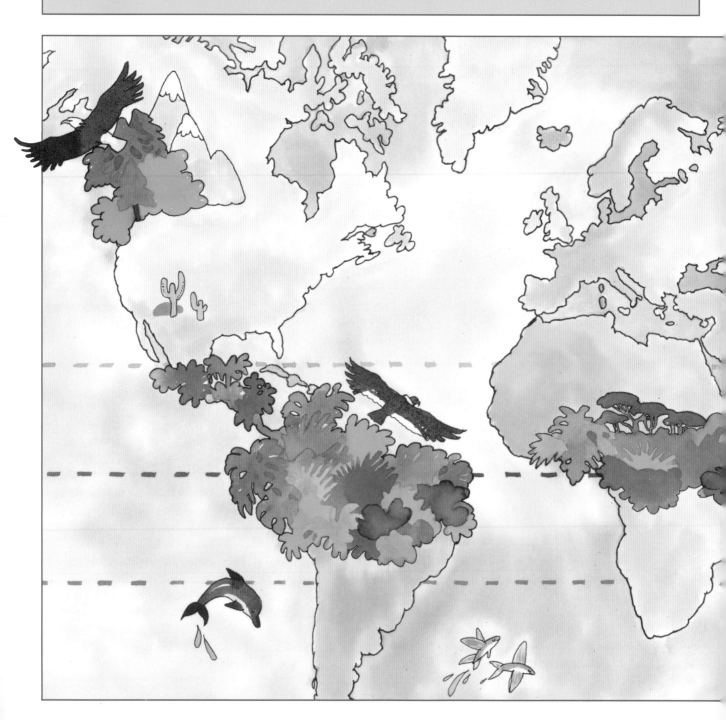

Why are people cutting down rain forests?

Rain forests are being cut down at the alarming rate of 100 million ha (250 million acres) a year. That's roughly the size of Great Britain! The trees are being cut for lumber and firewood, and to clear space to build homes, factories and roads, grow crops and graze cattle. They are also being felled to make it easier for miners to get at the minerals below the earth's surface. And some rain forest land is used for huge projects that produce hydro-electric power.

Why do rain forests need to be protected?

Rain forests are essential to the health of our planet. Here are just a few reasons why they need to be protected. They help combat the greenhouse effect by absorbing carbon dioxide from the atmosphere; they prevent soil erosion and flooding; they affect the world's climate by helping to keep temperatures more even, thus preventing searing heat and freezing cold; they are home to more than half of all the species of plants and animals in the world, many of which have yet to be studied; many rain forest plants produce valuable medicines; and last, but certainly not least, the leaves of the trees and plants produce oxygen that people and animals breathe. The Amazon rain forest alone produces almost 40 percent of the world's oxygen.

Where are the world's rain forests?

There used to be a lot more rain forest on Earth than there is now. Today it covers only 6 percent of the land surface of the world, down nearly half from its original extent. This map shows where rain forests are still standing.

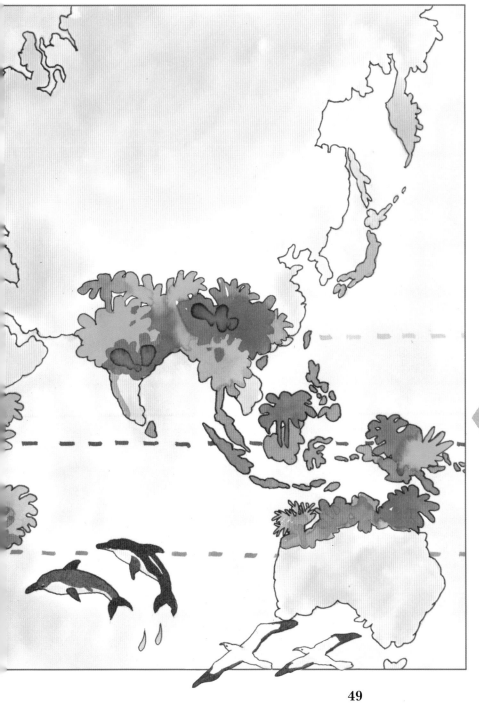

Don't rain forest animals mind all the rain?

Most don't because they have fur or feathers to protect them. But one—the orangutan that lives in the rain forests of Borneo and northern Sumatra—does make an effort to stay dry during a rain forest shower. It will often sit out tropical storms in treetop nests that it builds from branches and leaves. Apart from humans, the orangutan is the only creature that will build a roof over its nest or use leaves as a protective "umbrella" during a downpour.

What do orangutans eat?

An orangutan's favorite food is fruit, fruit and more fruit. In fact, it munches on more than 200 kinds of fruit and it spends over half its day eating them. If there isn't much fruit around, this ape will also eat leaves, bark, termites, ants and bird eggs. The orangutan gets its water from the plants it eats. But if it's really thirsty it will lick rain water from leaves and from its fur. It also "drinks" water it finds in tree hollows by dipping its arm into the water and licking the drops from its wrist.

Does an orangutan have any enemies?

Not many, although a hungry tiger or clouded leopard might take one on. And a young orangutan playing on the forest floor might fall prey to a large python. An orangutan's worst enemies are people—especially poachers and those who are logging the forests of Borneo for lumber. By cutting down these forests, people are making it difficult for the cautious orangutan to travel through the trees to find food. Without the rain forest, these apes will not survive.

How does an orangutan get around the forest?

Usually an orangutan swings through the forest relying on its long, strong arms, flexible joints and agile hands and feet to get around. But when it comes to a gap it stops and thinks about what it will do next. Unlike monkeys, who often jump from tree to tree, orangutans won't let go of one tree until they have a firm grasp on the next one. If the gap is too large, an orangutan sometimes bends a long branch over to make a link. A mother traveling with her baby may stretch herself out so that the baby can scamper over her to the next tree. But if it's a really big gap, the ape may weave a bridge from hanging vines and use it to make a safe crossing! When an orangutan wants to settle down to sleep, it finds a comfy fork in a tree and builds a soft, springy platform nest in which to curl up.

When you lose weight, where does it go?

Think of your body as a furnace that needs lots of fuel to keep running. Instead of coal or wood, you burn food and water. If your body gets more "fuel" than it needs, it stores it as fat—and that means extra weight. As you eat less food or become more active, your body starts to burn this fat. Think back to the furnace for a moment. As it burns coal or wood, its pile of fuel grows smaller. Fat also dwindles away as your body uses it up. It's broken down into carbon dioxide, water and energy. It leaves your body through your urine and sweat—and even in your breath.

Why do I get pins and needles when I sit on my foot?

When you sit on your foot, you pinch the nerves that carry electrical messages to and from your brain. Eventually, the flow of electricity through the nerve is completely blocked and you lose feeling in your foot. That's when you say your foot has "gone to sleep." You can wake it up by wiggling it. At first, your foot feels thick and fuzzy. Then it feels prickly, as all the nerve endings signal to your brain that they're waking up and starting to work again. But because they're all firing off messages at once, your brain gets confused and reads their signals as pain— "pins and needles."

Can you eat when you're standing on your head?

You can—but we wouldn't recommend it! It's easier to swallow when you're right-side up because then you've got gravity on your side. When you're upside down and gravity is working against you, your body relies solely on the muscles in your food canal, or esophagus, to squeeze the food up to your stomach. You'll enjoy your lunch a lot more if you sit down and relax.

What makes warts?

Warts are caused by the papilloma virus. Here's how it works. Like other viruses, the papilloma virus can't reproduce itself, so it invades the cells in your hands or feet and gets your cells to do the work for it. Cells infected by the virus divide and grow quickly until they end up piled on top of one another in that unmistakable warty shape. The good news about warts is that they always disappear. The bad news is that they're contagious and some kinds of warts may take longer to go away than others. So don't shake hands— or feet—with anyone who is a home to the pushy papilloma virus.

And by the way, don't worry about toads—you can't get warts from them.

Do animals use their heads?

Y ou bet! To find food, track each other down or even for show-ing off—animals put their heads to good use. Take a look at these head bangers, bone heads and other numb skulls.

Why do hippos have such big heads?

A hippo-sized head can be very useful for intimidating other hippos. Hippos roar when the sun comes up, grunt when danger is near and moo loudly enough to be heard 1 km (0.6 mi) away. But when it comes to fighting, a hippo would rather show than tell. And that's when a hippo uses its head. By opening its mouth in a wide yawn, a hippo threatens its opponent without having to spend much energy. If that's not enough to establish who's top dog, the hippo will rush at its opponent, bellowing all the way.

Do sea birds get headaches from plunging into the water?

Birds probably don't get headaches because they're specially built for their water dives. Take the gannet, for example. It plummets out of the sky and dives headfirst into the sea, searching for fish. How does it survive its 40 km/h (25 mph) dive? A gannet's head and brain are cushioned from the impact by an extra-strong skull and air sacs in its upper breast and neck that absorb the shock. The gannet has its own set of noseplugs, too. A special lid on its nose closes when it dives to prevent water from going up its nostrils.

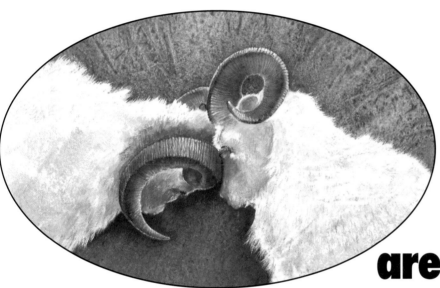

Why do rams bang their heads together?

Pretending not to notice each other, two dall rams turn away. Suddenly, they wheel around and charge full speed towards each other. Their huge horns meet with a thundering crash that can be heard more than 1.5 km (1 mi) away. What's going on? You've just watched a show of strength between two dall sheep during mating season. Some battles go on for hours but only rarely is a ram badly injured. Air inside its double-layered skull, as well as thick hair on the sheep's face, protect its brain and head like a hockey helmet.

What are the knobs on a giraffe's head for?

The next time you see a giraffe, take a good look at the horns on its head. A female giraffe has hairy tufts at the top of her horns while the male's are topped by bare skin. And a male's horns are larger than a female's. A female rarely uses her horns, but a male giraffe uses his to fight with other males for the right to mate with a particular female. A male giraffe swings his head against his opponent's neck, using his horns like clubs. To defend themselves against other animals, giraffes kick with their powerful legs instead.

Why is a human population explosion bad for animals?

◆

Until the last 100 years or so, people and animals have been able to live together fairly peacefully. There was enough room for people to build settlements, raise livestock and grow crops, while most animals were able to live safely in their natural habitats. Now things are changing, and fast. Ninety-three million people are born each year. It's no wonder we're having a serious effect on animals.

Lost Land

As more land is cleared for housing and for growing crops for food, the natural habitat of many animals is destroyed. Some animals are not able to adapt to their changing environment and they begin to die off. This world-wide problem has made many animals, including the African elephant, the Chinese panda, North America's eastern cougar and the cheetah that lives in Africa and Asia, endangered species.

Hunting and Poaching

Before people realized how quickly an animal can become endangered, many—like the sea otter—were hunted for their coats. Now, in countries where it is hard to make a living, some people have turned to poaching, which means illegally killing an animal. Elephants, for example, have been killed for the ivory of their tusks and jaguars for their coats.

56

Dangerous Waters

When huge tankers capsize and spill their cargo of millions of litres of oil, they create environmental havoc. So do fishing boats that use enormous drift nets. The nets, which are used to catch tuna and squid for people to eat, also snare and drown unsuspecting dolphins and sea birds.

Pollution, flood control dams and boat propellers in lakes and rivers have reduced a number of animals living in that habitat, such as the St. Lawrence beluga of Canada, to endangered status.

Garbage tossed carelessly into the water also can be deadly. Plastic six-pack rings, for example, can strangle fish and seabirds. And sometimes giant leatherback turtles swallow plastic bags thinking they are tasty jellyfish. The bag blocks the gut and eventually kills the turtle.

Pesticides

To combat the spread of crop disease, scientists developed pesticides, such as DDT. When DDT was discovered to be toxic, it was banned in North America. But it is still used in many developing countries where birds spend the winter. The peregrine falcon became endangered because it ate DDT-contaminated fish, insects and small birds. The high concentration of DDT in the peregrine's system caused it to lay eggs so fragile they broke under the mother's weight.

The Good News

It's not all bad news. Many concerned biologists are radio-tracking animals to learn where they go to feed, sleep and have their young. As we understand what the animals need, we can change our ways. And countries are working together to protect endangered animals. It's now illegal to hunt elephants, sea otters, beluga whales and many other animals, and there's an international ban on the sale of ivory in most countries. Also, the nesting areas of leatherbacks and the calving areas of belugas are being protected, reserves have been set up for cheetahs, elephants and pandas, and peregrines are being reintroduced into the wild. If we all make an effort, we will still be able to share this planet with these extraordinary animals.

Why would an owl want to live in the Arctic?

It's cold and there are no trees for nests or protection, so why would a snowy owl choose to spend most of its time up in the Arctic? Because it's full of food—voles, fish, arctic hare and even other birds. During the summer, the Arctic tundra also contains one of the world's most plentiful food supplies—lemmings. Fat and nutritious, these small guinea pig-like rodents are the perfect food for both adult and baby owls.

But every four or five years, when their population grows too big, lemmings leave their tundra homes in search of more food and living space. When that happens, snowy owls are forced to fly south to hunt for other food.

In the winter when the days turn dark, most snowy owls fly down to where there is some daylight. Some even head as far south as southern Canada.

Why don't snowy owls freeze to death?

It helps to be big if you're going to stay active during a cold northern winter because a large body makes more heat than a small one. It's no accident, then, that snowy owls are heavier and stockier than most other North American owls. And it's the female that takes the prize for size. With her wings fully extended, an adult female would reach from the front to the rear of your bike.

Being big isn't enough, however, to get the snowy owl safely through an arctic winter. It needs protective clothing too. Hard outer feathers act like a ski suit against the wind and snow. Underneath, the owl wears a "winter vest" of down feathers. These soft inner feathers trap body heat to form a layer of warmth. Feather-covered feet complete the snowy owl's arctic snowsuit.

Where do snowy owls build their nests?

When spring comes, the first thing any bird interested in raising a family has to find is a safe, protected nesting place. Usually owls nest in trees. But the tundra has no trees or any vegetation high enough to conceal a bird as big as an owl. So the snowy owl simply scrapes a shallow nest out of the earth and lines it with moss and feathers. Then she boldly settles down on it and, a few days later, starts laying eggs. This might sound crazy, but it's not. The female snowy owl, with her brown-tipped feathers, is well camouflaged for the tundra. That means she can hide her nest from predators such as birds and foxes that would love to steal her eggs. While she can see any predator approaching, chances are she won't be noticed.

How does a snowy owl swivel its head?

Unlike you, a snowy owl can't move its eyes in their sockets. Its huge eyeballs are held in place by a thin ring of solid bone. When it wants to look at something behind it, an owl turns its entire head. Extra bones in its neck allow the owl to turn its head backwards—a useful trick on the open tundra when you have to keep a careful watch for wily predators that like to sneak up from behind.

How does a snowy owl eat its food?

The snowy owl's sharp, curved beak is ideal for ripping up large prey, such as fish or arctic hare. Small prey are usually swallowed whole—something even three-week-old owlets can do. How? Flexible bones in the owl's lower jaw bend outwards and expand its wide mouth even wider. And backward-pointing barbs on the base of its tongue help move the food down the owl's throat.

Why can't I fly like a bird?

Have you ever wished you could soar and glide like a carefree bird? It's a dream most people share, but that's all it can ever be—a dream. You're simply not built to fly like a bird. Here's why.

Lighten Up

Birds, like cars, have most of their clever design features hidden. Teeth and jaws are too heavy, so birds have lightweight beaks instead. They also have bones that are almost hollow. Your solid bones account for about one-fifth of your body weight. A pigeon's bones, however, make up only one-twentieth of its total weight.

Redesign Your Body

Look at the shape of a bird. It's totally streamlined to cut down on air resistance. Its feet and legs tuck right up under its body, like landing gear on a plane. Where can you tuck your long legs, let alone your feet that stick out at right angles? As well, a bird doesn't have big ears to catch the wind like you have. To streamline your head you'd have to wear a swimming cap.

Reinforce Your Bones

A bird's bones may be light, but they are built to stand up to all the stresses of flying. Unlike your collar bones, a bird's collar bones are fused to form one "wishbone" that's strong enough to anchor all its flight muscles firmly in place. Also, birds have specially reinforced hip bones to help them take the shock of repeated landings. And the hollow bones of their wings are reinforced inside with lattice-like struts—like beams in a house—to make the wings stronger.

Grow Feather Muscles

Would gluing feathers to your arms help you achieve liftoff? Not a chance. While feathers would help the air flow by smoothly, they'd be useless to you without special muscles attached to them. In a bird's wing, each of its long, stiff primary feathers has its own muscle so that it can be twisted or turned to help the bird hover, zigzag or land.

Pump Some Iron

A bird needs powerful chest muscles to pull its wings up and down. Puny little chest muscles like yours won't do the trick. You'd have to work with weights until you're like a pigeon—up to half its total weight is in its enormous chest muscles!

By the way, not all birds can fly. The ostrich, for example, has heavy bones that support its weight as it walks around on the ground.

Does it rain in outer space?

Getting drenched in a sudden rain shower isn't a problem in outer space—it's too cold for water to fall. What's inside the clouds that are found out there? Instead of water, these clouds are made of hydrogen gas and dust. And some of them may be large—larger than our entire solar system! Instead of making rain, these clouds produce stars. One of the best-known stars, our sun, originally came from a cloud. So while there isn't any rain in outer space, you can think of stars as the "raindrops of the galaxy."

What's the biggest star in the universe?

Look at the southern sky on a clear winter's night and you'll see the constellation Orion, the hunter. It's easily identified by the three bright stars that form Orion's belt. In this constellation, you'll find the biggest star we know of in the universe. It's a red supergiant called Betelgeuse, an Arabian word that means "giant's armpit." And that's where you'll find it—in the hunter's armpit. How big is mighty Betelgeuse? It's so big that if it took the place of our sun it would engulf Mercury, Venus, Earth and Mars!

Do other planets have volcanoes?

The latest news on space volcanoes comes from NASA's Magellan project, an interplanetary space probe. Until now, much of the planet Venus was hidden by layers of clouds. But Magellan has been able to map out Venus's surface using radar images. These photographs show that the Venus landscape is marked by huge volcanoes, deep valleys and several enormous flat pancake shapes. Since much of the planet is covered in lava, some scientists believe that the volcanoes are still active. That may explain why the surface of Venus is much younger than the surface of Earth. It's a mere 400 million years old, one-tenth the age of our planet. But that doesn't mean Venus itself is younger than Earth. It could just mean that every few hundred million years Venus gets a new volcanic coating. Of the other planets, Mars has volcanoes, but they are no longer active. Mercury never had volcanoes and the other planets couldn't have volcanoes because they aren't solid. By the way, the place to go to watch volcanoes erupt is Io, the innermost of the four large moons of Jupiter. Volcanoes are constantly blowing on Io.

Index